Black History 365

African-American Life and Culture

3rd Grade Edition

Black History 365
African-American Life and Culture

Authors
Dr. Walter Milton, Jr. and Joel A. Freeman, Ph.D.

Co-Authors
Gabriella Williams-Hill
Dr. Alecia Beck Cobb
David Edgerson

Publisher
CGW365 Publishing
P.O. Box 151569
Arlington, Texas 76015
United States of America
blackhistory365education.com

ISBN: 978-1-7355196-8-5

23 24 25 26 LSBW 10 9 8 7 6 5 4 3 2

Cover Designer
Jasmine C. Cole

Layout & Design Team
Jasmine C. Cole
Joyce A. Evans

Chief Editor
Olivia M. Cloud

Academic Editor
Dr. Michele Hancock

BH365®
AUTHORS

DR. WALTER MILTON, JR., FOUNDER AND PRESIDENT OF BH365®, LLC

Dr. Walter Milton, Jr., is a native of Rochester, New York. He received his K-12 education from the Rochester City School District. He is a proud product of the State University of New York (SUNY) system. He earned a BA from the University of Albany and a MS from SUNY

College at Brockport. He took post-graduate courses at the University of Rochester to receive his administrative certifications, including his superintendent's license. He holds a Doctor of

Education degree in leadership and policy from the University of Buffalo.

Dr. Milton started his career in education in 1991 as a junior high school teacher for the Webster Central School District in Webster, New York and then Brighton Central School District a National Renowned School District in Brighton, New York. Dr. Milton has received numerous awards. Through the years, he moved from being a teacher, to principal, central administration and then to Superintendent of Fallsburg Central District, Fallsburg, New York. In 2005, he became Superintendent of Flint Community Schools, Flint, Michigan where he designed and implemented a district wide education reform that has been recognized throughout the State of Michigan and other parts of the country. He is the former superintendent in Springfield, Illinois, where he served as superintendent for almost eight years.

Dr. Milton is an inventor who holds a patent in addition to his academic and professional pursuits. Through his vision, he has had the ability to motivate educational organizations and communities to develop and support initiatives/programs that encourage students to achieve at their highest potential. He is a focused and disciplined leader with great vision, effective communication skills and a passion for students amid triumph or adversity.

Dr. Milton has also taught at several universities across the United States. He is also a published author of *Parents Perception of Schools and Schools Perception of Parents,* (2006), *Me in the Making – One Man's Journey to Becoming a School Superintendent* (2008), *Why Black Men Must Save Black Boys in America's Public Schools* (2014), *Truth Be Told-Narratives from The Souls of Black Women* (2018) and *Black History 365-An Inclusive Account of American History* (2020). Dr. Milton is currently CEO of Black History 365 (BH365®).

JOEL A. FREEMAN, PHD, CO-FOUNDER AND EXECUTIVE DIRECTOR OF BH365®, LLC

For 20 NBA seasons, Dr. Freeman served as player development mentor and character coach for the Washington Bullets/Wizards—surviving six coaching changes (1978–1998). Having grown up in Canada, it was during this period of time—working with NBA players—that his rather unique interest in Black history first emerged. In 1995, he co-authored *Return to Glory: The Powerful Stirring of the Black Race*. Basketball legend Julius "Dr. J" Erving wrote the foreword. Millions around the world have seen the film version of *Return to Glory* (available with Spanish, Portuguese, French, and English subtitles).

With travels to over 55 countries, Dr. Freeman has worked with the Association of International Schools for Africa (AISA), traveling extensively throughout the continent of Africa. He has also assisted in addressing issues surrounding conflict resolution, tribal warfare, and the AIDS crisis—meetings with over 100 African kings and queens throughout Benin, Togo, and Nigeria. He is in demand internationally as a motivational speaker and trainer for educational institutions, government agencies, non-profit organizations, and leaders of multinational corporations. Joel's presentation, *A White Man's Journey into Black History: An Eye-Opening Experience that Transcends Race,* has been well-received by audiences across North America.

The Freeman Institute® Black History Collection consists of well over 3,000 documents and artifacts (oldest date, 1553). At least a million visitors viewed items from the collection that were showcased at the United Nations headquarters in New York on two separate occasions. Other exhibitions have included: White House Communications, Secret Service, Clinton Presidential Library, Rutgers University, FBI, NSA, NOAA, NIH, EPA, Harlem Book Fair, NASA, NPR, NTSB, Howard University and many other venues.

Dr. Freeman has created at least 4,000 high resolution images from his collection. Many of those images appear throughout the pages of this BH365® textbook. [joel@blackhistory365education.com]

BH365
ADVISORY BOARD

Cathy Hughes
Founder and Chairwoman, Urban One, Inc.

Andrew Young
Civil Rights Activist, UN Ambassador

Dr. Rita Ali
VP, Illinois Central College

Pete Babcock
Historian, NBA General Manager

James Agbara Bryson
Great Grand Nephew of Annie Malone

Benjamin Crump
Civil Rights Attorney

Smokey Robinson
Internationally Acclaimed Singer-Songwriter

Dr. Marvin Dulaney
Historian, Educator

Jamila Thomas
Senior Vice President, Big Brothers, Big Sisters, Dallas

Robert Edison
Former Educator, Dallas ISD

Darrick Eugene
Finance Attorney & Lobbyist

George Fraser
Frasernet, FraserNation, Author

Patrick Gaston
Former President, Verizon Foundation

Paul Griffin
Former Vice President, Houghton Mifflin,
Past International President,
Phi Beta Sigma Fraternity, Inc.

Bill Haley, Jr.
Grandson of Alex Haley

Robert Jackson
National Education Speaker/Author

Alveda King
Niece of Dr. Martin Luther King, Jr.

Lewis Paul Long
Long Gallery, Harlem

Calvin Mackie, PhD
President, STEM NOLA, Inventor, Author

Kimberly Jones, Esq.,
Executive Vice President of the
Council for Opportunity in Education

Ben Watson
NFL Super Bowl XXXIX Champion

Mark Henry
WWE Hall of Fame, World's Strongest Man

James Page
Systems Analyst, New York State Bar Association

Loida Lewis
Attorney, Chair, Reginald F. Lewis Foundation

Arikana Chihombori-Quao, MD
Former Ambassador, African Union

Fadhilika Atiba-Weza
Exec. Dir., National Alliance of Black School Educators

Gordon Pennington
Former Dir. of Marketing, Tommy Hilfiger

BH365®
TEAM

Kimberly Bass
Carleen Brown
Reginald Braxton
Charlene Burroughs
Dr. Kevin "Khao" Cates
Dominick Clayton
Rev. Olivia M. Cloud
Jasmine C. Cole
Gloria J. Davis
Brian DeVeaux
Dr. Lisa DeVeaux
Barbara Spencer Dunn
Carlvern Dunn
David Edgerson
Aprill Edwards
Joyce A. Evans
Tim Fields
DeAndrea Fleming
Pam Freeman
Shirley L. Freeman
Stephen T. Freeman
Dr. Michele Hancock
Deneene Henderson
Connie Isabell
Earl A. Jones
Dr. Timothy Johnson
Rev. Charles Kearse
Tanisha Shorter Lott
Vickie Mitchell
Dr. Andrea B. Nelson
Shirley Ison Newsome
Lisa Joy Petros
Shawte Price
Andrae Rhyne
Dr. Caroline Ross
Martha Ross
Henry Sandoval
JoAnn Scaife
Ken Strickland
Lindsay Taylor
Bernard C. Turner
Roslyn Webb
Gabriella Williams
Dr. Marjorie Williams

Khairil Azhar Junos/Shutterstock

Shutterstock

BLACK HISTORY 365 EDUCATION

Shutterstock

Black History 365

African-American Life and Culture

BH365.Org

CONTENTS...

What's It All About? 10

CHAPTER 1: Our Origins: The Beginning of Our Story 14

CHAPTER 2: The Beginnings of African-American Culture 28

CHAPTER 3: African-American History and Culture Through Stories and Food 40

CHAPTER 4: African-American Language and Culture 56

CHAPTER 5: African-American Notables: Heroes and Heroines 68

End-of-the-Year History Makers Expo 88

Works Cited 89

Write 94

Shutterstock

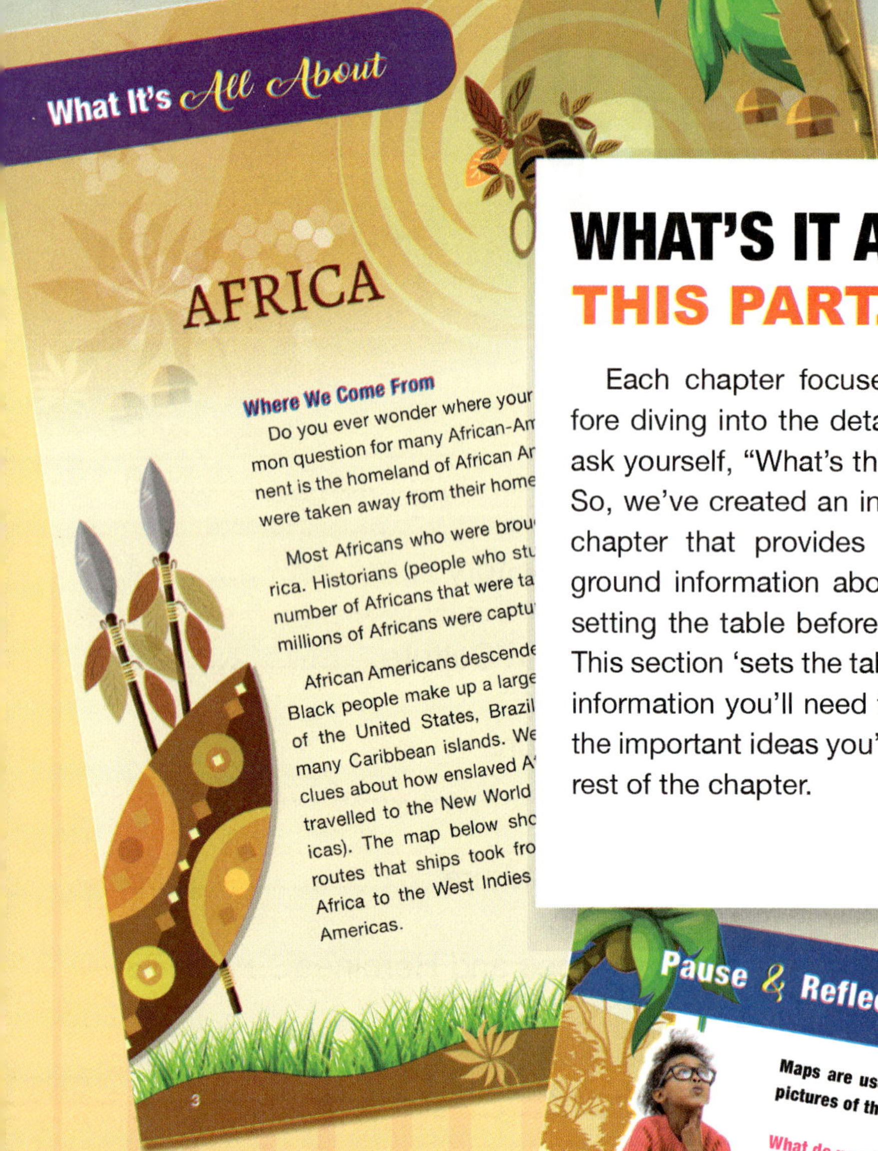

WHAT'S IT ALL ABOUT? THIS PART...

Each chapter focuses on one main topic. Before diving into the details of that topic, you might ask yourself, "What's this topic all about, anyway?" So, we've created an introductory section for each chapter that provides you with important background information about the topic. Think of it as setting the table before sitting down to eat dinner. This section 'sets the table' for you by laying out the information you'll need to access in order to digest the important ideas you'll read about throughout the rest of the chapter.

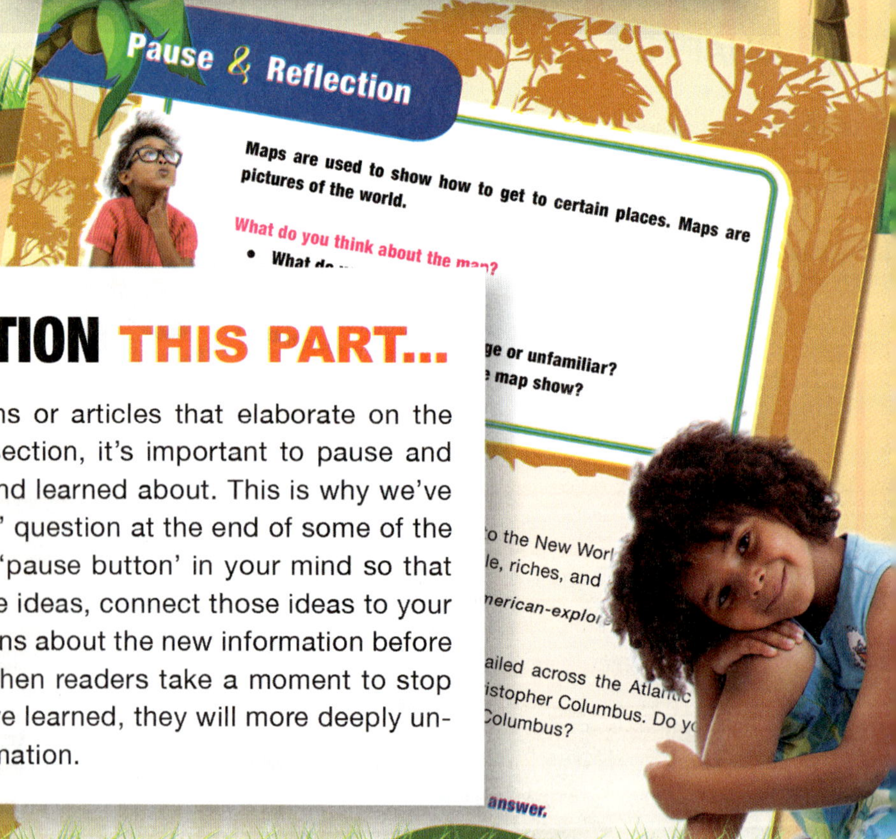

PAUSE & REFLECTION THIS PART...

Each chapter has several sections or articles that elaborate on the main topic. While reading each section, it's important to pause and think back on what you've read and learned about. This is why we've included a "Pause and Reflection" question at the end of some of the sections. We want you to hit the 'pause button' in your mind so that you can take some time to analyze ideas, connect those ideas to your own experiences, and form opinions about the new information before moving on to the next section. When readers take a moment to stop reading and reflect on what they've learned, they will more deeply understand the new ideas and information.

THINK ALONG THIS PART...

As you read the information in these chapters, you will interact with a lot of new concepts and ideas. Many ideas will form into personal thoughts or pictures in your mind as you think about them while you read. This is important to do; it will help you to better understand the material presented in this book. At the end of each chapter, you will find a section titled, "Think Along." It's designed to help you think through your own thoughts by:

- raising your awareness of connections you might make to your own experiences
- encouraging you to think critically about an issue or topic
- developing your ability to discuss your ideas with a classmate
- helping you to see that the information contained in this book isn't disconnected from your world, but rather is intertwined with your own lived experiences

WRITE ABOUT IT THIS PART...

One way to develop your ideas and new knowledge is to put your thoughts down on paper (or in a blog...). When you see a section titled, "Write About It," you'll find creative ideas for you to think deeply about an important topic in the chapter through writing. These writing activities are designed to provide you with authentic ways of communicating your new knowledge to the wider world. They'll provide you the opportunity to share your insights through creative formats and topics, all in an effort to extend your learning of the chapter's information.

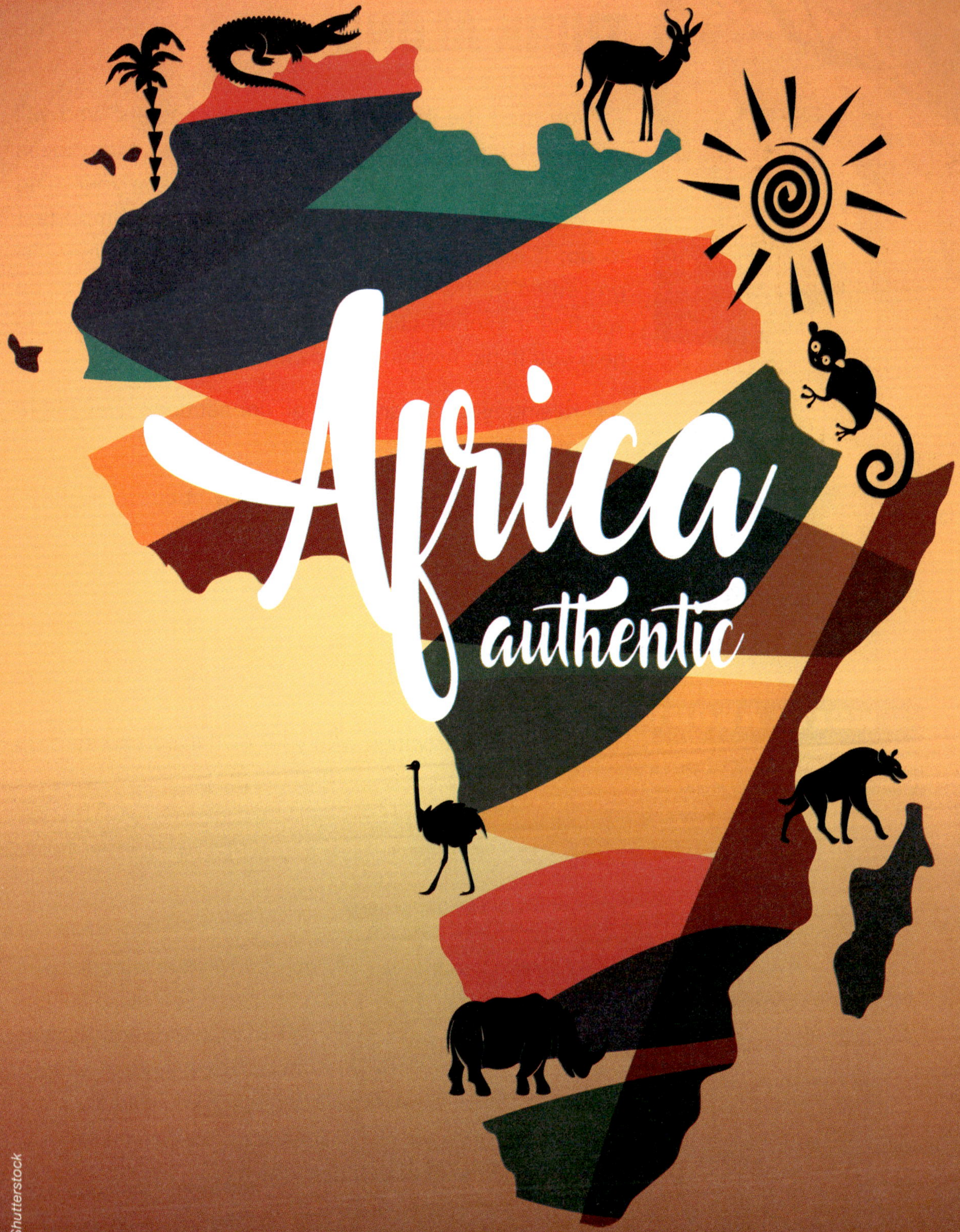

Shutterstock

GRADE 3

THE STORY:
AFRICAN AMERICAN
LIFE AND CULTURE

CHAPTER 1

OUR ORIGINS: THE BEGINNING OF OUR STORY

Shutterstock/ Rainer Lesniewski

MAP OF AFRICA

Vocabulary

African Gold Coast
the name for a region on the Gulf of Guinea in West Africa that was rich in gold

Ancestor
a relative or blood line from whom one is born; a parent, a grandparent, great-grand-parent, great-great grand-parent

Culture
The customs, beliefs, social forms, and traits of a racial, religious, or social group

Community
where we live, laugh, eat; spaces where we share things in common with other people

Church
where we worship, mourn, sing, and meet

Descendant
a person who comes from a specific ancestor

Enslave
to make a person a slave

Explore/Exploration
to investigate or study a place

History
the study of past events

Historian
a person who studies and writes about the past

New World
the Americas (North, South and Central America)

Proof
something that makes plain or clear

Slavery
a system in which another person owned one person

Trade
the action of buying and selling goods and services

Tradition
a belief or custom handed down from one generation to another

What It's *All About*

AFRICA

Where We Come From

Do you ever wonder where your family came from? This is a common question for Black children. The African continent is the homeland of African Americans. Many years ago, Africans were taken away from their homeland against their will.

Most Africans who were brought to America came from West Africa. Historians (people who study the past) do not know the exact number of Africans that were taken. But many historians believe that millions of Africans were captured.

Black people descended (came from) from enslaved Africans. Black people make up a large part of the United States, Brazil, and many Caribbean islands. We have clues about how enslaved Africans traveled to the New World (Americas). The map below shows the routes that ships took from West Africa to the West Indies and the Americas.

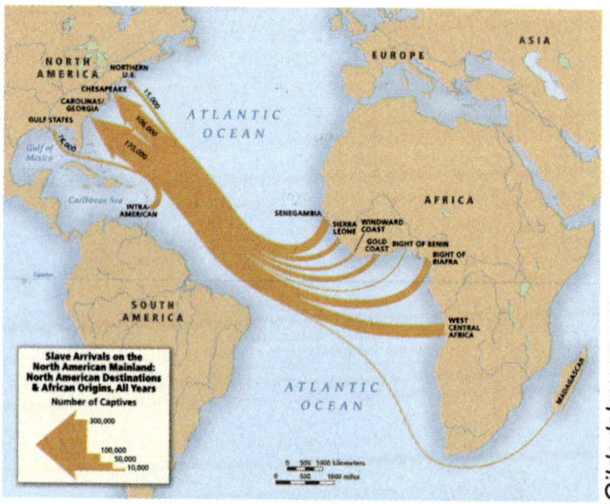

Map: Slave Trade from Africa to the Americas, 1650-1860

Africa is not a country. It is a very large continent that is home to 54 countries. In fact, Africa is the second largest continent in the world. It is so large you could fit the United States inside Africa four times! Being such a large continent, there are many groups of people who call Africa home.

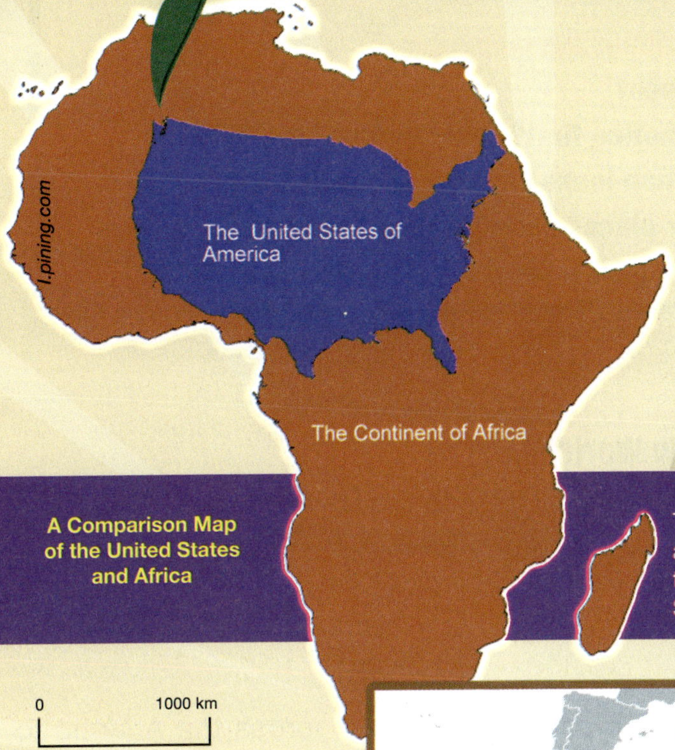

A Comparison Map of the United States and Africa

The continent of Africa is about four times larger than the country of the United States.

Pause & Reflection

Maps are used to show how to get to certain places. Maps are pictures of the world.

What do you think about the map?

- **What do you see?**
- **What do you notice first?**
- **What on the map looks strange or unfamiliar?**
- **What place or places does the map show?**

African Explorers to the New World

We know little about the African explorers to the New World. These brave African explorers discovered new lands, people, riches, and animals.

(https://blackexcellence.com/amous-african-american-explorers-youve-never-heard-of/)

Historians found proof that Africans often sailed across the Atlantic to the Americas. They sailed there even before Christopher Columbus. Do you think the Africans sailed to the Americas before Columbus?

Watch this video to discover the answer.

INTEGRATED TECHNOLOGY

African-American Explorers

The ancient Egyptians and West Africans traveled to the Americas long ago. They brought with them many skills and ideas. The Africans brought their knowledge of building pyramids, political systems, religious practices, mathematics, writing, and a calendar.

We have proof of Africans being in America before Columbus. This evidence (proof) came from papers written by Columbus himself. Columbus wrote about it in his diary. He wrote that the Native Americans told him, "black skinned people had come from the south-east in boats, trading in gold-tipped spears." (Christopher Columbus 1492. *(www.swarthmore.edu/SocSci/bdorsey1/41docs/01-col.html)*

The University of Almería, in Spain

Historians write that three African-Spanish brothers came with Columbus on his first voyage to the Americas in 1492. Pedro Niño was the pilot of the Santa Maria.

Although Pedro is a well-known member of Columbus's crew, he was not alone. Pedro's brothers Francisco (youngest) and Juan (oldest) were also part of these voyages (trips).

The early explorers in the New World included Africans. They came to the New World as explorers, servants, and slaves. (*https://legacysunfoldingjourney.blogspotAfrican.com/2013/07/african-explorers-and-settlers-of-new.html*) The Africans came to the New World as free people and servants to work on sugar, coffee, and tobacco plantations.

Enslaved Africans and free Blacks entered the New World along with the early explorers. Some of the **enslaved** people gained fame in the New World. Some also gained their freedom for helping to conquer the Americas.

Pause & Reflection

Did African explorers come to the New World? Was Christopher Columbus the first explorer to discover the New World?

Read About an African Explorer
Juan Garrido

www.accioncultural.es

We know little about the Spanish conquerors who came from Africa. Juan Garrido's diaries and records do tell us about his time exploring the New World.

Juan Garrido was born around 1480 on the West Africa coast. He arrived in Lisbon as a free person when he was a teenager. Many historians believe that he was the son of an African king or merchant who knew Portuguese traders.

In 1503, Juan traveled from Seville to Puerto Rico and Cuba with a team of explorers. During this expedition (a trip to explore), they were unable to defeat the native people who lived there and on nearby islands.

In 1513 and 1521, Garrido made two trips to Florida. Later he served in the Spanish army. After leaving the army, Garrido settled in Mexico City. He became the caretaker of the city's water aqueduct (a canal for water to flow from one place to another).

Juan Garrido and Hernán Cortés (another Spanish explorer) meeting Aztec people in Mexico

Visit St. Augustine

Pause & Reflection

What have you learned about the African explorers in the New World? Use your journal to write three interesting facts you learned about African explorers.

The Enslaved African-American Family

Captive Africans created a "family unit" from those taken to South America or the Caribbean before being taken to North America.

In the New World, some captive Africans created families in America through marriage, childbirth, and adoption. But there was always a risk that a family member could be sold or traded away.

Enslaved Africans tried to keep their families together. Families provided a form of protection for the members of the community. Many children whose parents had been sold were taken in by other enslaved families. Being enslaved made having a family life hard.

Enslaved women did most of the house work, cooking, cleaning, and childcare.

Folklife/bighouse

Most enslaved people could not legally marry in any American colony or state. Colonial laws considered enslaved people to be property or goods, like a horse. Most African Americans could not legally marry until after 1865, when slavery ended in the United States.

Many enslaved Black couples wanted to recognize their union, anyway. In the South, many enslaved people "jumped the broom" as a type of wedding ceremony. The broom was an important part of wedding ceremonies in Ghana. Enslaved Africans kept this tradition to the United States.

Enslaved people lived as a community. On large plantations, the yards around the slave cabins served as a community center for enslaved family members. They used these common areas when they were not working. Enslaved people held celebrations in their community areas.

Many enslaved people also were not allowed to worship among themselves. Instead, they often held prayer meetings in the woods where the White slave owners could not hear them.

Enslaved parents and elders taught children lessons on loyalty. They taught the children how to treat people. Elders also told children stories about their family history. The threat of being separated was always a concern for enslaved people. They valued family time because it could easily be taken away from them. You will learn more about how they used the community areas in chapter two.

Wikimedia Commons

Slave quarters, Mulberry Plantation, South Carolina.

A Black family enslaved Africans

Library of Congress

Pause & Reflection

What have you learned about the early African Americans and their lives in the New World?

Storyblock

Storyblock

THINK *Along*

How do you think you would feel if your family was enslaved?

Would you try to leave or would you stay and work on a plantation?

WRITE ABOUT IT

After reading about enslaved family life, write a story with a beginning, middle, and end that describes a day in the life of an enslaved family.

Storyblock

Nathaniel Tetteh / Unsplash

CHAPTER 2

THE BEGINNINGS OF AFRICAN-AMERICAN CULTURE

Nathaniel Tetteh / Unsplash

Vocabulary

Folktale
a belief or story passed on orally from one generation to another

Proverb
a general saying expressing commonly held ideas and beliefs

Griot
An African tribal storyteller and musician

Genealogist
a person who traces or studies where people have come from. In African culture, genealogists keep up with the births, deaths, marriages, and history

Adapted
to adjust or change to fit different conditions, a new environment

Elder
An older person; a person having authority because of age and experience

Culinary
something related to food, cooking, or the kitchen

Storyblocks

What It's *All About*

AFRICA

How Is Culture Passed Down?

The culture of people can be expressed in many ways. African-American culture has been preserved and passed down from generation to generation. Before history was written, it was kept alive in stories and folktales. These stories were passed down orally.

Jay-Z: African American Rapper

Shutterstock/ Adam J. Sablich

The culture was passed to the next generation. Each new generation learned the food, religion, and music of their heritage (where they came from). African-American culture is expressed through hairstyles, dress, dance, art, food, cultural celebrations, and language.

From chapter one, we learned about the origin and history of enslaved Black people in the New World. In chapter two, we will discuss cultural traditions they brought with them, how they were passed down from generation to generation, and how they changed over time.

JEKESAI NJIKIZANA/AFP via Getty Images

African Storyteller

We will begin exploring African-American culture through its rich oral traditions.

Storytelling and Folktales

Folktales have played an important role in how African American culture has been kept and passed down. Folktales are stories that became a tradition among a group of people or **folk**. Stories and messages were passed down through storytelling or through songs. Their messages were expressed as folktales, fables, and proverbs.

A proverb is a short saying, usually familiar to many people. The proverb is wise words or advice about life. By telling stories, Black people made sense of their world. They used stories to teach lessons, values, and history.

African-American folktales and proverbs have roots in Africa. They were **adapted**, (changed) to apply to their lives in America. People living in different parts of the country had different ways of doing things. The folktales were adapted to fit their unique ways.

The stories told the knowledge, beliefs, and values they brought from Africa. By adapting their storytelling, they were able to cope with their harsh treatment in the New World. Storytelling was a way to remember their experiences and tell them in this new land without causing trouble.

Favorite Folktales

Most African-American folktales explain how things came into being. Folktales taught life lessons by telling stories. Some stories were about trickery and trouble. Some stories were about victory over evil. Other tales were funny while others were funny ghost stories. Some stories were about the enslaved and their slave-owners.

One of the most popular trickster folktale characters were the stories of Brer Rabbit and Anansi, the spider. These folktales were funny. Tricksters were animals who could talk and play tricks on others. But each tale taught a valuable lesson.

Shutterstock/Deep Green

Oral Storytelling in the African Village

Children loved to sit and listen to the elders (older adults) as they sang and told stories. Children gathered to listen to stories when it got too dark for them to play or do their chores. This tradition, known as Tales by Moonlight, began in Africa.

Many folktales teach moral lessons such as kindness, honesty, or loyalty. There is usually a hero or heroine and a villain. They provide examples of the problems that can happen to people who don't have these qualities. *Mufaro's Beautiful Daughters* is an old African folktale that remains very popular today.

Pause & Reflection

What is a folktale? Do you know any African-American folktales?

Proverbs: Teaching Life's Lessons

A proverb, or parable, is a wise saying. Proverbs are short sayings used to share important messages to children and adults. Proverbs are usually short sentences with a powerful meaning. They cause people to think about their meaning and apply it to a life situation.

Images.app.goo

Think About It

Read this proverb and reflect on its meaning. Discuss with a partner.

"The best way to eat an elephant in your path is to cut him up into little pieces."

What does it mean?

Images.app.goo

This proverb has been adapted many times. When someone faces a big problem, the proverb is posed as a question and answer. For example, "How do you eat an elephant? One bite at a time!"

Can you think of a time when you were faced with a huge concern? How did you solve your problem?

African Proverb and Sayings to Live By: "How Do You Eat an Elephant? One Bite at a Time." Illustration by Williams Warren

African Proverbs

Africa has many proverbs. There are thousands that come from all cultures and countries. They are unique to each region and tribe. African proverbs are part of the oral tradition, just as folktales, songs, oral histories, and poems.

Proverbs help to keep customs and values. They also teach lessons. Through proverbs, we can learn about the wisdom of African Americans. The wisdom comes from their African heritage and from their experiences in American life.

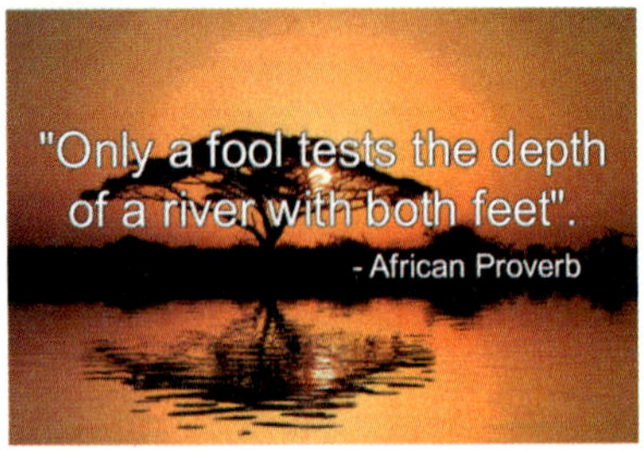

Images.app.goo

African Proverb and Sayings to Live By "Only a fool tests the depth of a river with both feet."

Other African Proverbs:

"Unless the lion learns to write their own story, the hunter will always be the hero."

"If you are filled with pride, then you will have no room for wisdom."

"Love and smoke are two things that cannot be concealed."

"An enemy does not sleep."

"The eagle does not hunt flies."

"Do not call the forest that shelters you a jungle."

"If you want to go fast, go alone. But if you want to go far, go together."

Images.app.goo

African Proverb and Sayings to Live By: "Until the lion has his own storyteller, the hunter will always have the best stories."

African-American Proverbs

Over the years, Blacks have adapted many proverbs and created others. Their proverbs apply to their life here in America. Some proverbs have stayed true to the original version. Others have not. Still, proverbs continue to teach lessons on good behavior, good judgment, and wisdom. African-American proverbs also give war

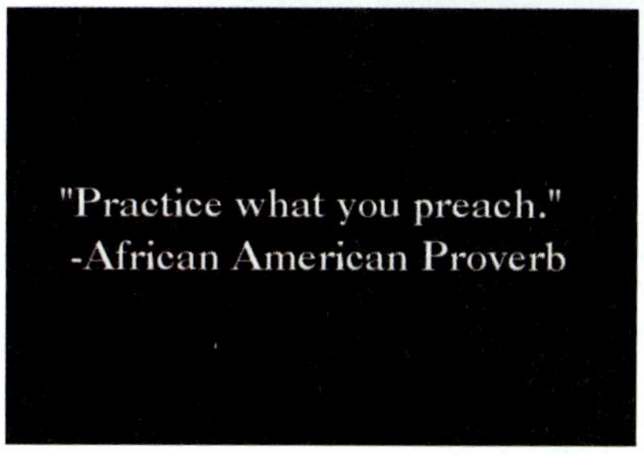

Images.app.goo

African American Proverb
"Practice what you preach."

Many sayings deal with topics such as love, jealousy, strength, wealth, and laziness. The figures or characters in the proverbs can be humans, animals, nature, or spirits. Such proverbs are often used when correcting children's behavior or warning adults. There is a proverb that applies to just about every life situation. Following are examples of African-American proverbs:

"An empty wagon makes a lot of noise."

"A hard head makes a soft behind."

"The fruit doesn't fall too far from the tree."

"Don't bite the hand that feeds you."

"Beware of burning your bridges when you cross them."

African-American Proverb

"God helps those who help themselves."

Images.app.goo

American Proverb:
"If you think you are too small to make a difference you haven't spent a night with a mosquito."

THINK Along

Compare African American proverbs to the African proverbs you learned.

What differences do you notice?

WRITE ABOUT IT

Click on the link. Listen to the story. Use a Venn diagram to compare/contrast the characteristics of Mufaro's two daughters. What lesson can be learned from this story?

INTEGRATED TECHNOLOGY

Mufaro's Beautiful Daughters

Akturer / Shutterstock

CHAPTER 3

AFRICAN-AMERICAN HISTORY AND CULTURE THROUGH STORIES AND FOOD

Akturer / Shutterstock

AFRICA

Chapter three will explore how African-American storytelling and food tell the Black experience in the United States. African Americans are descendants of storytellers. You will learn that storytelling was combined with food to connect Black Americans to culture and traditions.

Griots: The Power of African-American Storytelling

Proverbs and storytelling are a means of teaching lessons and giving advice. It is a cultural tradition that requires a lot of skill. In West African culture, a person who tells stories is called a 'griot' (gree ow).

A griot's job is vital because they do a lot more than tell stories. Griots are the 'official' storytellers, historians, advisors, musicians, praise singers, poets, and genealogists. A genealogist is a person who traces or studies where a family or group comes from. Genealogists are responsible for keeping up with births, deaths, and marriages in the village or town.

Griots are sometimes called *Jalis*. They used their gift of music, instruments, and poetry to entertain, share history, and give advice.

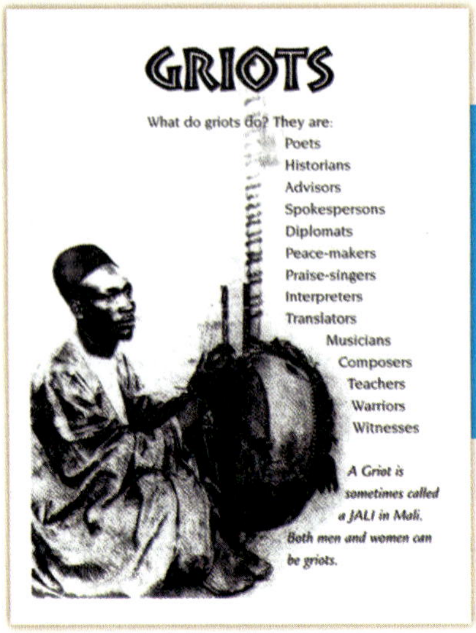

Images.app.goo

The Job Description of a Griot

Read the job description of a griot in the picture. Imagine, griots began this oral tradition before there were any written records. There were no storybooks. There were no history books to read and study. There were no written records of the thousands of proverbs used to give advice.

Musicians did not have sheet music to help them play or sing. There were no written records of births, deaths, or marriages in families. How did they do it?

Not just anyone could be a griot. Village griots were born into a griot family. It took many years of special training to learn the many stories, proverbs, songs, and history.

Griots could be male or female, but they were usually male. Their training started at around 8 years old until they were 18 years old. The griot's main job was to entertain the villagers with skilled storytelling. The stories held life lessons. These stories shared their knowledge of history, values, and culture.

Griots were a vital part of the village social life. The griots usually did not charge money when they performed. However, people in the audience would often give them money to thank them.

Adriana Bouhid, Member of Ujima Group of Black Storytellers

Rioonwatch.org

Go to the link and listen to the video. Take the quiz to see how much you know about griots.

INTEGRATED TECHNOLOGY

Griots Quiz

Storyblock

Pause & Reflection

Discuss the job of a griot and the challenges griots faced. What questions do you have about griots?

Akturer / Shutterstock

Do Griots Still Exist?

Yes! There are modern-day griots in Africa and America. The art and practice of storytelling are making a return. It is once again becoming a popular art form.

The term "modern griot" applies to both African and African-American griots. They are living storytellers, oral historians, musicians, singers, poets, advisors, and genealogists.

Remember, to be a griot you must have a griot in your family ancestry. Modern griots often begin their performances by paying tribute to their ancestors. They will call the ancestors names.

The audience plays a critical role in storytelling. The audience shows approval and appreciation. They clap, sway to the music, shout praises, and repeat phrases or chants.

The griot comes dressed in beautiful, colorful clothes that help build curiosity. The drummers, musicians, and dancers help get the audience in the mood for storytelling. The griot performs like an actor sharing wisdom and knowledge.

Shutterstock

The Griot's performance is full of emotion, humor, and expressions, such as shouts and screams.

Rhythmic language such as poetry and song is a part of their storytelling. Many Black griots tell the traditional African folktales passed down from generation to generation. A popular African folktale is "Why Mosquitoes Buzz in Peoples' Ears." Others tell African-American folktales, such as "The People Could Fly."

Today, both African and Black American griots have adapted storytelling traditions to include political and social injustices. Some of the newer forms of storytelling sound a lot like rap.

Chapter four will explore how storytelling has changed using various forms of music, from spirituals to rap. Some storytelling includes spoken word, which is a new form of poetry often recited with music.

The griot tradition is a part of African-American culture. Two griot museums have been established in the United States to honor the storytelling tradition. One museum is in Atlanta, Georgia. The second museum is located in St. Louis, Missouri.

Pause & Reflection

Click the hyperlink to the Griot Museum of Black History of St. Louis. Read about its history and mission, and take the virtual tour.

INTEGRATED TECHNOLOGY

Griot Museum of Black History

The Food of the Enslaved to Soul Food

Culture can be passed down through food and ways of cooking. For enslaved Black Americans, food was not just about passing on cultural traditions. It was also about survival. These cooking traditions remain popular, but they also are a reminder of difficult times.

The enslavement masters gave their enslaved the unwanted portions of meat. The enslaved took the unwanted meat and made tasty dishes from them. Today, some of those cuts of meat are popular dishes.

When enslaved Africans were captured and brought to the New World in the 1600s, the traders also brought several crops native to Africa. They brought okra, sesame seeds, peanuts, black-eyed peas, and rice. The enslaved Africans also brought their styles of preserving, seasoning, and cooking these traditional foods.

The enslaved Africans were given only a tiny portion of food each week. They learned to make tasty dishes with undesirable cuts of pork and beef, cornmeal, and vegetables. The undesirable cuts of pork included the head, feet, internal organs, ears, and "fatback" from the hog. They boiled leafy greens such as collards, the green tops of beets and turnips, and wild weeds for vegetables.

Corn was an abundant crop in the South. It was the most common ration for the enslaved. Several dishes, such as cornbread and grits, were made from dried and boiled grains from corn. These are still popular today.

To stretch the small amounts of food given, enslaved Africans planted small gardens with seeds from their native land. After working in the fields, they also fished and hunted.

Molasses was used as a sweetener in their dishes and drinks. Molasses is thick, dark syrup made from sugarcane or sorghum (a type of grain).

Black Americans were able to create meals and ways of cooking that became a Southern tradition known as soul food. Now, it is an American tradition.

Soul Food

Images.app.goo

Soul Food: A Plate Of Ham Hocks, Greens, Black-eyed Peas, and Rice

When we hear the term "soul food," our mouths may water. We may think about crispy fried chicken, barbecue ribs, creamy macaroni and cheese, greens, sweet potatoes, and cornbread. Other soul food dishes include gumbo, jambalaya, fried okra, and black-eyed peas. Black Americans have passed down their recipes for hundreds of years. The history of these foods tie African American culture back to its African origins.

Shutterstock

Southern Cuisine: Fried Chicken, Collard Greens, Cream Corn, and Black-eyed Peas

Soul food comes mainly from the Deep South. The Deep South states include Louisiana, Alabama, Mississippi, Georgia, and South Carolina. That is why soul food is now referred to as Southern cuisine. It is one of the most popular types of food in the United States.

What is your family's favorite "soul food" meal?

Glacee / Shutterstock

Soul Food: BBQ Ribs with Coleslaw and Potatoes

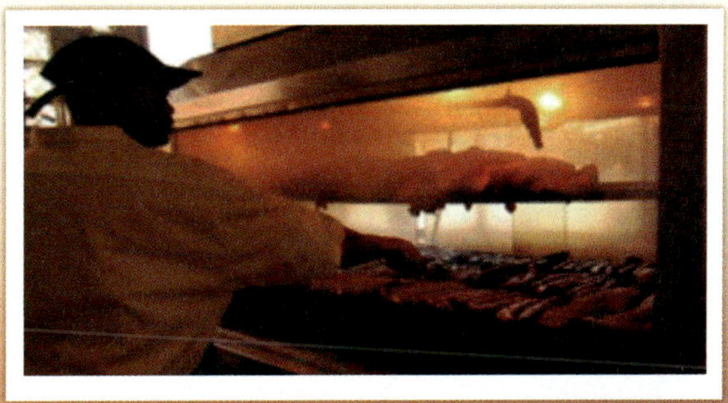

Blackfoodie

Smoking Meats in the Southern Tradition

Pause & Reflection

Traditional African-American food is an excellent way to study and explore African American history and culture. It is one of the only ways African Americans keep their connection from Africa to present-day America.

Barbecue

Barbecuing is a tradition rooted in the Deep South. During the period of enslavement, there were no refrigerators. Enslaved African Americans had to pour large amounts of salt on their meats and smoke them using wood and low heat. This process would make the meat last for long periods.

Enslaved Blacks created ways of preserving meat that became very popular. They used different types of wood to add flavor when smoking meat. In the Deep South, pork was the main choice of meat.

Images.app

Soul Food: Pork Ribs, Greens, Macaroni and Cheese, and Cornbread

Pause & Reflection

Barbecuing is still a big part of family gatherings and celebrations. When was the last time your family had a gathering or a backyard cookout? What do you like about family cookouts? What cookout activities and traditions does your family have?

THINK Along

Soul Food: Origins of Soul Food

Libguides

Black-eyed Peas

Black-eyed peas are actually beans. They are a light tan color with a black eye in the center. Black-eyed peas are related to cowpeas or field peas that are native to Africa. Cows ate the stems and vines after the corn crops had been picked. A tradition among many African Americans is to eat black-eyed peas on New Year's Day to bring good luck.

Chitlins

Libguides

Chitterlings, or "chitlins," are a Black American culinary tradition. Chitterlings are the small intestines of the pig. They must be cleaned very well before they are cooked. Today, many consider chitterlings to be a delicacy (very special dish).

Cracklin' Bread

Libguides

Corn (maize) was ground into cornmeal to make cornbread. There are different ways to make bread from corn, like hoecakes and hush puppies. Cracklin', or crackling bread, is cornbread with bits of fried pork and fat in it. This bread is usually cooked in a skillet to make the cornbread crispier.

Libguides

Greens

Some common greens eaten in West Africa include okra and akatewa (a kind of spinach). Some of the greens that are popular in soul food are collard greens, mustard greens, turnip greens, and kale.

Libguides

Okra/Gumbo

Okra is the main ingredient in gumbo, a spicy stew or soup that is a tradition in Louisiana. Other ingredients often used include vegetables mixed with chicken, pork, shrimp, or crawfish. The stew is thickened with okra or a powder made from sassafras leaves.

Gumbo and other types of Creole foods have their origins in the colonial era. The cuisine is a blend of African, Native American, and European dishes. The word "gumbo" comes from the African word for the vegetable okra, *quilombo*.

THINK *Along*

Libguides

Molasses

Southerners used molasses to sweeten food and beverages. Blackstrap (very dark) molasses was a tradition in African American cooking. It is made by slowly cooking the juice of sugar cane. Sorghum syrup, similar to molasses, is also made by cooking the juice of the sorghum plant. It is believed that African captives brought sorghum seeds with them and grew it in the South.

Libguides

Peanuts

Peanuts are the same as groundnuts in Africa. The Portuguese brought peanuts to Africa. The enslaved used peanuts to make pies and soups.

Libguides

Rice

Captives from West Africa, a rice-growing region, were brought to the South to work on the rice plantations of South Carolina.

THINK Along

Libguides

Sweet Potatoes

Yams are not sweet potatoes. In the South, however, sweet potatoes are often referred to as Louisiana yams. West African yams are tubers (the thick part of the plant that grows underground). They are more similar to potatoes than sweet potatoes.

Libguides

Watermelon

Watermelon was cultivated from the native African vine *Citrullus lanatus*. It may be eaten as a dessert or used in recipes. The fruit can also be used to make pickled watermelon rinds or preserves. Africans used the sweet juice from the watermelon. They boiled it down to make syrup. In the deserts where watermelons grow, the juice is used instead of water during droughts.

What is culture?
What are some ways culture is passed down?
What is an important cultural tradition in your family?
Why is it important?
What happens when the culture is not passed down?
What is a special dish that has been passed down from older generations in your family?

WRITE ABOUT IT

From the African Table to Your Table

Soul food is from the South. It is basic home cooking that has been passed down through the generations. Because these recipes have been passed down, many cookbooks today feature African American recipes.

Enslaved Africans used food to tell stories and pass down traditions. In African American culture, cooking was seen by many to be a form of freedom.

A lot of soul food is often made up of peas, beans, greens, cornmeal, and pork. Cornmeal is used for cornbread, hush puppies, johnnycakes, and seasoning for fried fish. Pork was a staple (main ingredient) in cooking. African Americans used pork in many ways, including seasoning vegetables, making stews, and pickling.

"Hoppin John" is a popular African American recipe. This vegetable dish is made with black-eyed peas and rice. Another traditional dish is macaroni and cheese, made of macaroni, cheese, and added spices from the West Indies.

In your journal, write about your family's favorite "soul food" meal. Then, to add to your story, interview family members about their favorite dishes. Ask who taught them how to cook the dish. Then find out how they got the recipe.

Antonio Chico / Shutterstock

CHAPTER 4

AFRICAN AMERICAN LANGUAGE AND CULTURE

Antonio Chico / Shutterstock

Vocabulary

Creole
a person of mixed European and Black descent, especially in the Caribbean. A form of speaking made from two languages.

Descendants
coming from an ancestor.

Dialect
a form of a language that belongs to a specific region or social group. "This novel is written in the dialect of Trinidad."

Diaspora
the scattering of people in large groups from their original homeland.

Ebonics
the language of all people descended from enslaved Africans, mainly in West Africa, the Caribbean, and North America.

Geechee
an English creole language spoken by some Black people in parts of South Carolina and Georgia. A person who speaks Geechee.

Gullah
a member of a Black community living on the coast of South Carolina and nearby islands. Speaking Gullah is a mix of English with West African languages.

Blues
an African American music form that started in the Deep South around the 1860s. The blues were created from work songs and spirituals.

Genre
a specific type of music, film, or writing.

Gospel
music is deeply rooted in the African American church. It is a genre of Christian music with powerful vocals and harmony. Gospel music evolved after Emancipation.

Jazz
a type of music that started with Black America. Jazz blends gospel music, brass bands, African music, blues, and Spanish music.

Negro Spirituals
the Spirituals (Negro Spirituals or African American spirituals) is a form of music that came from African Americans' experiences with slavery and oppression.

Origin
beginning or start.

Ragtime
a musical genre that enjoyed popularity between 1897 and 1918. Some believe ragtime got its name from its ragged rhythm.

Rap/Hip Hop
the performer chants or says words that rhyme. Hip hop lyrics are often about life in large cities. Hip hop uses musical styles from other genres such as disco, R&B, and reggae.

Reggae
this genre that began in Jamaica in the late 1960s and remains popular in Jamaica today.

Rhythm & Blues (R&B)
R&B became very popular in African American communities, starting in the 1940s.

Zydeco
a style of Black American dance music originally from Southern Louisiana.

AFRICA

How Did Enslaved People Communicate?

This chapter deals with how Black Americans developed various ways of communicating. Here we will explore two important forms of communication. One type is the spoken language. The second type is the lyrical/musical language.

The Language of Enslaved Africans

Have you heard that America is a "melting pot" of different people? A melting pot is when all people try to understand, honor, and accept cultural differences. The United States has no official national language. However, many countries have an official language. At least 350 languages are spoken in the United States today.

African captives came to America from many different regions and spoke different languages. They did not have a common language. As a result, they had to speak and use English as a common language. Most of them blended parts of their native language with the English they learned.

INTEGRATED TECHNOLOGY

What are some of the colorful languages used by African American descendants throughout the United States? Let's think about and discuss just a few of the more widely-known dialects. **Click on the links to hear the dialects**.

- Creole Louisiana Creole Woman speaking Louisianese Creole French Interview | Louisianese French
- Gullah Hidden History: Speaking Gullah
- Geechee Gullah: Geechee Code-Switching
- Ebonics What America Got Wrong About Ebonics

Shutterstock

Pause & Reflection

Why do you think that language patterns differ from region to region in our country?

The Origins of Creole Language

The Creole language comes from a mixture of people. These people were of French, Spanish, African, and Caribbean descent. Many settled in the Southern Louisiana area.

Creole is a term that generally describes people of mixed ancestry, mainly colonial French, African American, and Native American.

The term Black Creole refers to freed slaves from Haiti and their descendants. Creole is Haiti's official language, along with French. There are some differences between French and Creole, but they sound the same to the average listener.

The Origins of the Gullah Language

The Gullah people are descendants of Africans from Sierra Leone. The Gullah are a Black Americans who settled in the Carolinas and Georgia from the West Caribbean. Gullah people farmed the rice plantations and fished on islands off the coast of South Carolina and Georgia. Because of their isolation on these small islands, the Gullah people held on to their language and culture.

The Gullah people mixed their native language with English. This allowed the Gullah to communicate with English-speaking people.

The Origins of the Geechee Language

The Geechee language comes from the Low Country. This region includes parts of the Georgia, Florida, and South Carolina coastal areas. The Geechee language also developed in the rice fields, mixing colonial English and African languages.

The Gullah and the Geechee terms are often used to mean the same thing. Examples of words and phrases of the Gullah-Geechee language include:

- Cootuh (turtle)
- Oonah (eat)
- Buckruh (white man)
- Swonguh (proud), and
- Benne (sesame)

Pause & Reflection

Do you think African American language will continue to change? If yes, how would the language change?

The Origins of the Ebonics Language

The word Ebonics is a blend of the words "ebony" and "phonics." Ebonics was identified in 1973 by an African American named Dr. Robert Williams. The use and study of Ebonics is still debated today.

"Ebonics" means "Black sounds." Ebonics represent slang words such as "phat" for excellence and "bling" for flashy jewelry for many people. Lots of people use these words, not just Black people.

Other Ebonics terms have stayed within the Black community. The term "kitchen," describes the curled hairs at the base of the neck. The word "ashy" is used among Blacks to represent the look of dry skin. These terms have been around for decades, but are largely unknown outside of the African-American community.

Ebonics also replaces standard English words with others (i.e. replacing the word "beginning" for the term "fixin' to" or "fin' to").

Ebonics words and phrases are not spoken in the same way as the English language. Certain words and phrases sound different due to Black dialect. They also sound different by the dropping of some consonants and the way vowels are spoken.

The words sometimes sound different due to the altered verbs and tenses. This is common in other languages as well.

Ebonics is not poor grammar. It is another spoken language of Black Americans. Ebonics tells how Black people developed a different language after being separated from their original languages.

Pause & Reflection

Would you like to speak a different language? Do you think languages are still being developed today?

Communicating the African American Story Through Music

Another form of communication occurred through song. Music was added to the songs using homemade tools or instruments, such as washboards, spoons, wash tubs, etc.

Communicating Through Song

Spirituals and gospel are musical patterns that did not happen by accident. They have evolved through the Black American experience.

This music began with the struggle of the captured African people who were shipped to the Americas (and throughout the world). Those kidnapped people were able to develop a code system. This system was helpful during slavery. Blacks would sing what became known as Negro Spirituals to express their pain and their hope.

These spirituals eventually evolved into what became known as gospel music. Traditional gospel is very emotional. It tells hopeful news to those singing as they praise and worship God. Since then, the creativity of Black people has shifted from gospel music into other forms. These shifts include today's gospel rap, and gospel hip hop.

Black music genres came about over time. As they evolved, these Black music genres had an impact on other forms of music. For example, rock' n' roll was influenced (shaped) by the blues, which came from Black musicians in the Deep South.

In 2001, singer Little Richard told Time Magazine that, "Rock'n' roll started as rhythm and blues. There wasn't nobody playing it at the time but black people — myself, Fats Domino, Chuck Berry!"

https://www.vibe105to.com/tuned-in/where-rock-nroll-came-from

Certain styles of music came from African spirituals, African chants, work songs, field hollers, rural fife and drum music, and church hymns. The blues grew out of the Mississippi Delta not very far from New Orleans, the birthplace of jazz!

Early jug bands (music made by playing a jug, or container) used many types of musical instruments. These bands used jugs, guitars, mandolins, banjos, kazoos, stringed basses, harmonicas, fiddles, washboards, and other everyday appliances made into crude instruments.

Jazz started in the Black communities of New Orleans, Louisiana, in the late 19th and early 20th centuries. Jazz has its roots in blues and ragtime.

Some of the notable African American pioneers of ragtime and blues are:

- Mike Bernard (1875–1936)
- Ben Harney (1872–1938)
- Scott Joplin (1868–1917)
- Jelly Roll Morton (1890–1941)
- Tom Turpin (1871–1922)

Notable African American Musicians

George Washington Johnson

Americanchampions365

Can you name any Black musicians? Have you ever heard of George W. Johnson?

George W. Johnson was born enslaved. He became the first Black musician to sell the records he made. Johnson sold thousands of his recordings.

Today, the Library of Congress salutes George W. Johnson's for his music. His recording, "The Laughing Song," has been added to the National Recording Registry. The National Recording Registry is a list of important sound recordings that reflect life in the United States.

Click on link:
The Laughing Song - George W. Johnson (1898)

INTEGRATED TECHNOLOGY

The Laughing Song

INTEGRATED TECHNOLOGY

Zydeco a Pas Sale

Click the link: "Zydeco a Pas Sale", Jeffery Broussard & the Creole Cowboys

Musical genres (or categories) often influence one another. It can be hard to tell where one genre begins and where one ends. Gospel blends into the blues. The blues blends into jazz and ragtime. The blues mixed with a Creole influence and style is called zydeco.

Zydeco is enjoyed in many of the Southern parts of Louisiana. Recently, it has made its way into neighboring states such as Texas and Alabama.

Other forms of music are found mainly in certain parts of the country. Go-Go music is popular in Washington DC, while house music is most often heard in Chicago.

Each form of music has its unique way of sharing messages. That is how the language of music has grown over the years. Over the years, many popular songs have had coded (hidden) messages. When the enslaved shared a secret thought, they placed it in the lyrics of a song. Messages were hidden in spirituals or work songs.

Pause & Reflection

Why are there different types of music? What type of music would you like to learn more about?

THINK *Along*

America's music is rooted in the Black community. The enslavement-era spirituals about struggle, the blues, jazz, and hip hop started in America. Understanding music provides a wonderful way to celebrate African American history. You have read about the African-American music, musicians, and writers that contributed to the American story.

Listen to the spiritual.

How does hearing the spiritual make you feel?

INTEGRATED TECHNOLOGY

Lift Every Voice and Sing

WRITE ABOUT IT

African-American music teaches about the struggles and bravery of the people. Today, Black singers and songwriters continue to shape American music. Do you have a favorite African-American singer or group? Who is it? Write three sentences about why that is your favorite singer.

____

____

____

Yaayi / Shutterstock

CHAPTER 5

AFRICAN-AMERICAN NOTABLES: HEROES AND HEROINES

Vocabulary

Abolitionist
a person who wants to end the practice of slavery

Accomplishments
good things people have achieved

Caldecott Honor
an award for artists' pictures in a children's book

Excelled
did exceptionally well (at something)

Farmer's Almanac
book with calendars and writings about the seasons and the best days to do outdoor activities

Harlem Renaissance
a celebration of African American creativity and life in a neighborhood in New York City

Honor
credit for acting well or doing good deeds

Invention
a new or original creation

Legend
a very famous person

Notable
a famous or important person

Obstacle
something that stands in the way of (or stops) progress

Obstacle
something that stands in the way of (or stops) progress

What It's *All About*

AFRICA

Our Heroes and Heroines

There have been great Black Americans throughout history. Black legends like Benjamin Banneker, Harriet Tubman, Sojourner Truth, Frederick Douglass, and Dr. Martin Luther King, Jr. were famous civil rights heroes and heroines. There are many more from the past and others in the present.

Black Americans have helped shape what America is today, but not just by the Civil Rights Movement. Black writers, inventors, doctors, artists, athletes, and others have made a difference in America.

Chapter five will introduce Black American heroes and heroines who have contributed to this country. You will find out more about Black Americans who changed history, achieved greatness, and made an important mark on our culture.

Well-Known Enslaved Black Americans

Benjamin Banneker (1731–1806)

Benjamin Banneker taught himself how to read and write. He was a scientist, astronomer, inventor, and writer who spread the word against slavery. He built a clock made entirely from wood. He also wrote a book called a **farmers' almanac**. He was one of the first Black Americans to gain honor for his achievements in science.

Benjamin Banneker's Amazing Clock

INTEGRATED TECHNOLOGY

Benjamin Banneker

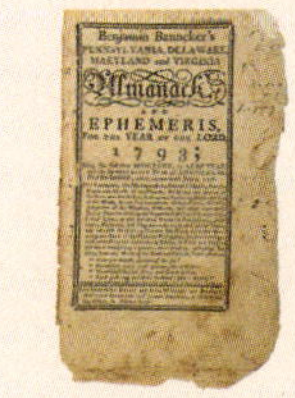

Benjamin Banneker's Farmer's Almanac

U.S. National Archives and Records Administration / public domain

Public Domain

Booker T. Washington (1856–1915)

Booker T. Washington was born enslaved in Virginia. He was a very smart man who founded a college that is now called Tuskegee University. He also started the National Negro Business League.

In 1872, Washington left home and walked 500 miles to go to college. He took odd jobs to support himself. The college let him attend the school. He took a job as a janitor to help pay for college. The school's headmaster, General Samuel C. Armstrong, helped Washington to finish his schooling.

Booker T. Washington became famous for his conflicts with other Black leaders. He argued with W. E. B. Du Bois about the best way for Black people to get ahead. Booker T. Washington is remembered today as the most important Black American speaker of his time. *(www.biography.com/activist/booker-t-washington)*

Shutterstock

Harriet Tubman (1820–1913)

Harriet Tubman was an enslaved woman who escaped to freedom. She later became a "conductor" on the Underground Railroad. She led enslaved people to freedom before the Civil War. She was also a nurse and a spy for the Union Army. She was a strong supporter of women getting the right to vote.

Tubman is one of the most important people in American history. Her bravery has inspired people from every race and background.

Harriet Tubman was born around 1820 on a Maryland plantation. Her parents named her Araminta Ross. She later changed her name to Harriet to honor her mother. Harriet's mother had worked as a cook in the plantation's "big house." Her father was a timber worker. Harriet had eight brothers and sisters, but many of them were scattered by slavery.

The American Wanderer / Shutterstock

After gaining her own freedom, Tubman led more than 300 enslaved people out of bondage. She made at least 19 trips to the South to free more people. Each time she came back South, she put her own life in danger. Her heroism to free as many enslaved people as she could earned her the nickname "Moses." *(www.biography.com/activist/harriet-tubman)*

Military Times

William H. Carney in Uniform

William Harvey Carney (1840–1908)

Sergeant William Harvey Carney was born near Norfolk, Virginia in 1840. His parents were enslaved, but their owners had promised them freedom. Carney grew up enslaved. He was secretly taught to read and write by a local minister. He was later set free and became a soldier during the American Civil War.

Carney quickly moved up in rank to become a sergeant. On July 18, 1863, he took part in the Union Army's assault on Fort Wagner in Charleston, South Carolina. He became the first Black soldier granted the Medal of Honor. *(www.norfolk.gov/3256/William-Harvey-Carney)*

Notable African American Inventors

Alexander Miles, Designer of the Modern Elevator

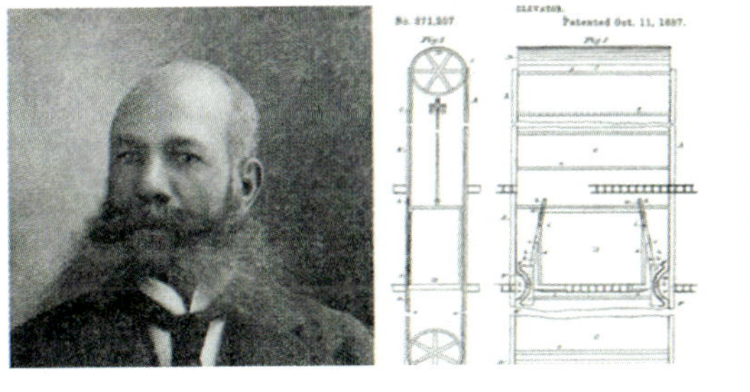

Chocolatevent

Alexander Miles (1838–1918)

Alexander Miles invented a tool that made the elevator and its shaft safer to use. Miles received a patent for his design for improving the way elevator doors opened and closed. Before his invention, elevator doors were opened and closed by people. If anyone forgot to close the shaft door, passengers could fall into the shaft and be hurt or killed. The shaft housed the elevator inside. *(www.invent.org/inductees/alexander-miles)*

Elijah McCoy, "The Real McCoy"

Public Domain/Henry Ford Museum

Lubricating Cup

Elijah McCoy (1844–1929)

Elijah McCoy liked taking items apart and putting them back together. McCoy wanted to improve how trains run. McCoy improved how trains were oiled so they could run smoothly. He developed a "lubricating cup" that could drip oil when and where needed to grease the train engine.

His invention helped trains to run smoother on tracks. The lubricating cup was a great success! Railroad companies from all over the country used McCoy's lubricating cup. Other inventors tried to say their cup was just as good. Railroad companies soon learned that McCoy's was the best. They would say, "I want the real McCoy." *(https://blackinventor.com/elijah-mccoy)*

Public Domain

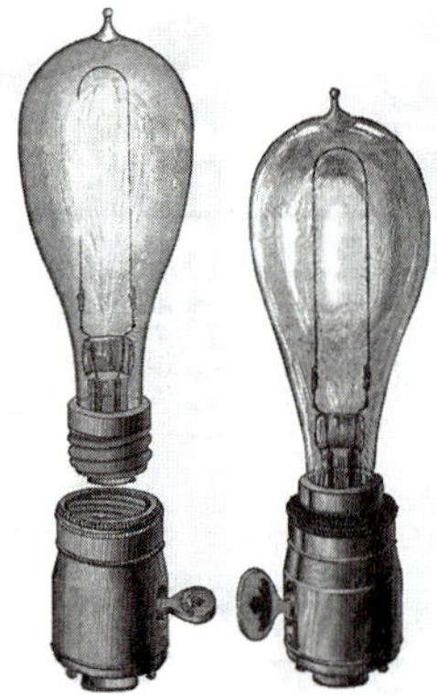

Lewis Latimer (1848–1928)

Lewis Latimer had many inventions. He is famous for his work on electricity. Latimer created a long-lasting filament (a thin metal thread) for the electric light bulb. He also helped Alexander Graham Bell obtain the patent for the first telephone.

Latimer was in great demand for his scientific knowledge. His invention helped make electric lighting a common use in our homes today. *(www.thoughtco.com/lewis-latimer-profile-1992098)*

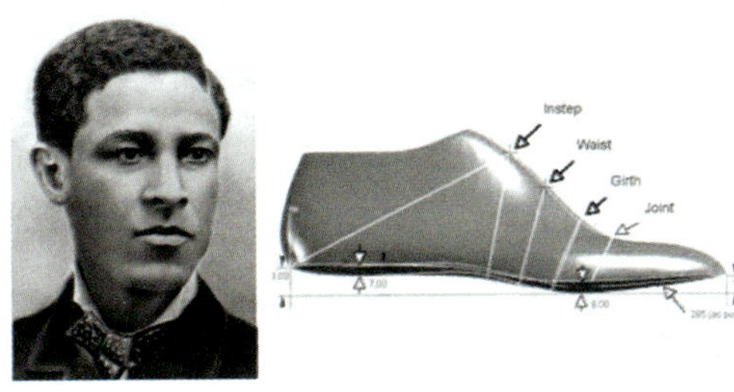

Invent.org

Jan Ernst Matzeliger (1852–1889)

Jan Ernst Matzeliger came to the United States at age 20 from Paramaribo, Suriname, a small country in South America. He ran a shoe-stitching machine for a factory in Lynn, Massachusetts. In those days many people could not afford to buy shoes because they cost a lot of money. Matzeliger worked on his own time to invent a shoe lasting machine.

In 1883, Matzeliger invented the shoe lasting machine. Many before him had tried, but couldn't do it. The machine quickly attached the top of the shoe to the sole. This process is called "lasting."

Matzeliger's machine could produce ten times as many shoes as human hands could create in a day. This invention changed the shoe making industry and made shoes affordable for more people. *(http://teacher.scholastic.com/activities/bhistory/inventors/matzeliger.htm)*

INTEGRATED TECHNOLOGY

Honoring Jan Ernst Matzeliger

Library of Congress

George Washington Carver National Monument

George Washington Carver (1864–1943)

George Washington Carver was most likely born enslaved in Diamond, Missouri. Like many enslaved children, the exact year and date of his birth are unknown. Carver was one of many children born to Mary and Giles. They were an enslaved couple owned by Moses Carver.

Carver studied plants at the Iowa Agricultural College (now Iowa State University). In 1896, Booker T. Washington recruited Carver to teach at Tuskegee Institute's Agriculture School. There, Carver taught a groundbreaking crop rotation (turning) method.

The South desperately needed the new farming technique. Carver urged planting cotton one year, then peanuts or sweet potatoes the next. This helped the soil to build up new minerals. Southern farmers followed his lead and had great success. The farmers were able to grow a large peanut supply that many used to feed animals.

Carver also developed more than 300 uses for peanuts. He made products like ink, hand lotion, and cooking oil. Many people believe that he invented peanut butter. This is a myth. Still, Washington did help to make the food popular. *(www.history.com/topics/black-history/george-washington-carver)*

Chris Higgins Photography / Shutterstock

Madam Walker Family Archives

Madam C.J. Walker (1867–1919)

Sarah Breedlove was born in 1867. By the 1890s, she was having trouble with hair loss. Hair loss was a common problem for Black people. Since indoor plumbing was not in many homes, people did not wash their hair often. Walker experimented with different homemade hair treatments until she found something that worked.

She learned a lot about hair while working for Annie Malone, a Black woman who owned a cosmetics business. In 1905, Sarah moved to Denver, Colorado to work as a sales agent for Malone. She also married Charles Joseph Walker.

After changing her name to "Madam" C.J. Walker, she founded her own business. Her first hair product was "Madam C.J. Walker's Wonderful Hair Grower." She traveled around the country to sell her products and give hair care advice to African American women. Madame C.J. Walker was very good at selling her hair products. She became very wealthy and owned many homes. She is one of America's first self-made female millionaires.

(http://teacher.scholastic.com/activities/bhistory/inventors/walker.htm)

Bloximages

Garrett Morgan, Sr. (1877–1963)

Garrett Augustus Morgan, Sr. was an inventor, businessman, and community leader. In 1914, Morgan invented a "safety hood." It made polluted (foul) air more fit to breathe. His invention was an early version of the gas masks later used in World War I. During the war, the masks protected soldiers from poison gas.

Another important invention by Morgan was the traffic signal. Garrett's invention warned drivers when to stop their cars. One day he saw an accident between a horse carriage and a car. After that, Morgan wanted to solve the problem and make driving safer.

The US government honored Morgan for his traffic light invention. Morgan's inventions and service made all people's lives better and safer. Traffic signals are still helping people drive safely today. *(www.biography.com/inventor/garrett-morgan)*

Marie Van Britton Brown (1922–1999)

Wikimedia/U.S. Patent and Trademark Office

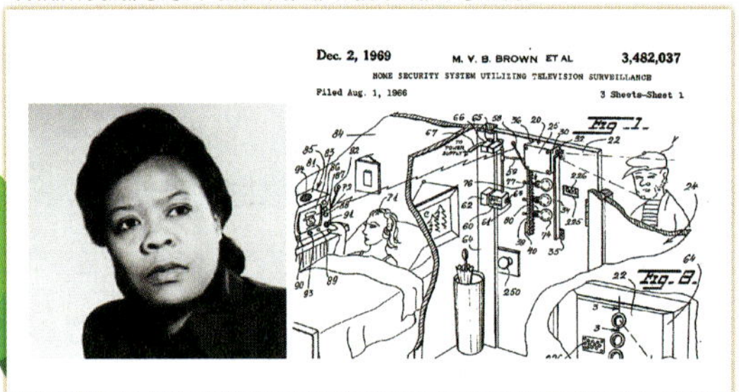

Marie Van Brittan Brown lived all of her life in New York. She was a medical nurse concerned about safety in her community. She and her husband worked late hours. Crime in her community was a problem. Police were slow to come after a crime was reported. Brown wanted to make her home safe.

Marie, with help from her husband, invented the first home security system. The patent for the invention was filed in 1966 and received in 1969.

Today's home security systems are based on the Browns' invention. Her invention is still used by businesses, small offices, single-family homes, and apartments. *(https://lemelson.mit.edu/resources/marie-van-brittan-brown)*

IBM

Mark Dean
(1957–)

After college, Mark Dean worked for a well-known company as a computer scientist. He helped to invent the IBM personal computer and the color monitor. He also created the technology that allows devices, such as keyboards, mice, and printers, to be plugged into a computer and talk with each other. After making a computer that was smaller and affordable, Mark worked with other designers to make computers faster and hold more information.

Because of Dean's work, many people have a computer in their home today. *(www.biography.com/inventor/mark-dean)*

INTEGRATED TECHNOLOGY

What's Your Big Idea? - Mark Dean

Notable Civil Rights Activists

The United States Senate

Hiram Revels
(1827–1901)

Long before the Civil Rights Movement grew stronger in the 1950s, Hiram Revels did great work to improve life for Black people. A minister and Civil War veteran, Revels was the first Black man elected to the US Senate. As a senator, he fought for Black and White students to attend the same schools. He also fought for equal rights for African American workers. *(https://history.house.gov/Exhibitions-and-Publications/BAIC/Historical-Essays/Keeping-the-Faith/Civil-Rights-Movement)*

INTEGRATED TECHNOLOGY

Reconstruction: The Vote - Hiram Revels

National Parks Service

Nannie Helen Burroughs (1879–1961)

Nannie Helen Burroughs was an educator and civil rights fighter. She was once denied a teaching job in Washington D.C. for being "too dark." Burroughs decided to set up the National Training School for Women and Girls in Washington. This school helped Black high school and college-aged women learn skills other than cooking and cleaning. Burroughs believed that women needed an education and job skills. She also wanted Black and White women to work together for the right to vote.

Burroughs died in 1961. The school she set up for Black women is now named after her. *(https://bestlifeonline.com/civil-rights-leaders)*

The National Archives

Mary McLeod Bethune (1875–1955)

Mary McLeod Bethune's life was almost like Burroughs' story. They were both educators and civil rights fighters. They both opened schools to improve the lives of African American girls and women.

Bethune's school became a college to show women how to become teachers. Her school later joined with a men's college to become Bethune-Cookman College. She also founded the Negro Council of Women in 1935 to help fight for equal rights for African American women. (*www.womenshistory.org/education-resources/biographies/mary-mcleod-bethune; www.tampabay.com/florida-politics/buzz/2018/03/20/5-things-to-know-about-mary-mcleod-bethune-whos-getting-a-statue-in-the-u-s-capitol)*

Wikimedia Commons

National Archives

Bria Goeller

Ruby Bridges
(1954–   )

Ruby Bridges became a symbol of the Civil Rights Movement. In 1954, the Supreme Court ruled in *Brown v. Board of Education* that all American children can have an equal education. This meant Ruby would be able to go to the school very near her home. Before the court ruled, Ruby went to kindergarten far away from her home. At age 6, Ruby was sent to William Frantz Elementary School in New Orleans, which had been a school for White children.

On her first day, she had to be taken to school and protected by federal agents. A famous painting by Norman Rockwell titled, "The Problem We All Live With" shows little Ruby being led to school.

Some White people were very angry. They did not want Ruby to attend school with White children. They shouted hateful words at her as she walked to school. Most of the teachers stayed out of the school and refused to teach. Many White parents kept their children home from school. They did not want their children attending school with a Black child.

As Ruby grew older, she began to understand her important role in history. She was the first Black student to attend school with White students because of a court ruling.

Ruby's parents had the strength and courage to fight for equal rights under the law. Ruby's bravery is why today Black and White children can learn in the same classrooms. *(www.womenshistory.org/education-resources/biographies/ruby-bridges)*

INTEGRATED TECHNOLOGY

The Story of Ruby Bridges

Notable African American in the Arts and Literature

Public Domain/Wikimedia

Carter G. Woodson (1875–1950)

Carter G. Woodson was an American historian. He is known as the "Father of Black History." Woodson started the celebration of Negro History Week. The one-week celebration later became Black History Month.

In 1915, Woodson co-founded the Association for the Study of African American Life and History, Inc. **(ASALH)**. The group works to educate people about African American history and culture.

Woodson was also founder of *The Journal of Negro History* and *The Negro History Bulletin*. In 1920, he founded the Associated Publishers, Inc. The publishing company printed works that other companies would not. Some companies would not publish writings from Black scholars and women. They also would not publish books on how African Americans were stolen from Africa and packed on unsafe ships.

Carter G. Woodson stood up for women, too. Woodson treated African American women as equal co-workers and leaders. Most male scholars did not treat women as equals in those days. Mary McLeod Bethune was the first woman elected president of ASALH in 1936. She remained president until 1952. *(www.nps.gov/cawo/learn/carter-g-woodson-biography.htm)*

Asalh.org

INTEGRATED TECHNOLOGY

Journal Bulletin

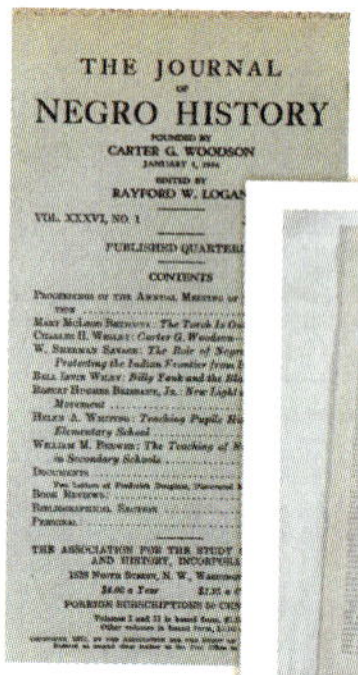

Smithsoinanmag

Public Domain

Jorge Salcedo/Shutterstock

Phillis Wheatley (1753–1784)

Phillis Wheatley was the first African American to write and publish a book of poetry. She was born in West Africa. At the age of 7 or 8 years old, she was sold into enslavement and taken to North America in 1761. John Wheatley, a wealthy tailor from Boston, bought the little girl and named her Phillis Wheatley. Phillis became the personal servant to John Wheatley's wife, Susanna.

Susanna and her daughter, Mary, taught Phillis to read and write English. With her creative writing, Wheatley showed that she was just as intelligent as Whites.

Wheatley's first poem was published in 1767. She had become widely known by 1770. Wheatley did not write much on the topic of enslavement in her poems. Still, her best-known work is "*On Being Brought from Africa to America*," written in 1768. *(www.womenshistory.org/education-resources/biographies/phillis-wheatley)*

Everett Collection

Frederick Douglass (1818–1895)

Abolitionist (a person who wants to end slavery) Frederick Douglass was born into enslavement around 1818 in Talbot County, Maryland. He became a famous political thinker and civil rights leader. He advised presidents and gave speeches to thousands of people about different causes.

Douglass wrote about his life in books. When a person writes about their own life, it is called an autobiography. He described his life during enslavement and his life after the Civil War. *(www.biography.com/activist/frederick-douglass)*

Jacob Lawrence (1917–2000)

Wikiart.org

Jacob Lawrence was the first Black American artist to have his work shown at the Museum of Modern Art in New York City. He received praise and awards for his artwork. He also received other medals and awards for his work. To learn more about Jacob Lawrence's life and work, view the video from the link. *(https://lawrencemigration.phillipscollection.org/artist/about-jacob-lawrence)*

Wikiart.org

Wikiart.org

INTEGRATED TECHNOLOGY

Jacob Lawrence brief Biography and artwork

Kathy Willens/AP/Shutterstock

Faith Ringgold (1930–   )

Tar Beach Book Cover

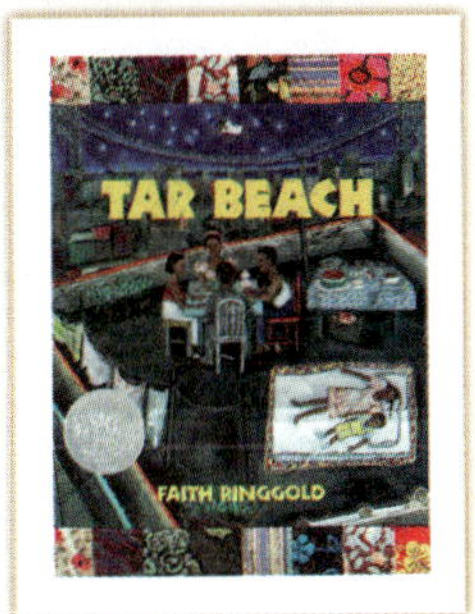

Faith Ringgold is a famous African American artist and author. She is known for her story quilts. A story quilt is made with pictures, sound, scents, cloth, and textures that are used to tell a story.

Ringgold used fabric and canvas to tell about the lives and history of Black Americans. In 1991, Ringgold created a children's book titled, *Tar Beach*. The book tells about a young Black girl who wishes to fly. She received the Caldecott Award for her book in 1992.

She wrote other books like *Aunt Harriet's Underground Railroad in the Sky* and *My Dream of Martin Luther King* to help children learn about African American history. *(www.serpentinegalleries.org/whats-on/faith-ringgold)*

INTEGRATED TECHNOLOGY

Faith Ringgold reads her 1991 children's book Tar Beach

Carnegielibrary.org

Langston Hughes (1901–1967)

Have you ever heard of the word "essay"? An essay is a short writing that tells the writer's opinion (views). In 1926, Langston Hughes wrote an essay, "The Negro Artist and the Racial Mountain." This essay spoke to Black society and culture. It also started the **Harlem Renaissance**.

Hughes wrote, "We younger Negro artists now intend to express our dark-skinned selves without fear or shame."

Hughes published more than 35 books. To learn more about Langston Hughes, watch Caleb with Curls as he tells why Hughes was so special to the African American community. *(www.biography.com/writer/langston-hughes)*

INTEGRATED TECHNOLOGY

Langston Hughes and the Harlem Renaissance video for kids: Black History Heroes: Caleb with Curls

THINK *Along*

How do people become famous? Name the talents or actions of the African Americans in this chapter that made them famous.

Would you want to become famous? What are your talents?

WRITE ABOUT IT

Pick an African American person from this chapter. You also can pick someone who you want to learn more about.

Draw a picture of the person you chose. Write two facts about the person. Share your picture with the class and tell why you chose the person.

____

____

____

____

____

____

____

____

____

BLACK HISTORY 365 EDUCATION

Putting It All Together: End-of-the-Year History Makers Expo

As you end this year's study of BH365®, it's time to celebrate your work! Did you know that by engaging in this course of study you are making history? The activities you engaged in and the topics you discussed are artifacts of history never seen before.

To celebrate your efforts, the BH365® content creators have organized an End-of-the-Year BH365® History Makers Expo.

To prepare you will:

- Review the artifacts of the work you completed throughout the course of study.
- Select one that you believe should be shared with the world.
- Create a presentation to share your selection that includes:
  - An introduction explaining why you chose this artifact.
  - The artifact you selected.
  - Detailed information on the artifact from your presentation
  - A conclusion that includes your thoughts on what you hope people will learn from the artifact.
  - Create an artifact collection of all entries your class plans to submit.
  - Collaborate as a class to determine the chronological order in which to place each presentation to ensure the viewing audience experiences the artifact collection in a manner that represents its historical context.
  - Get directions from your teacher for uploading the presentation to *blackhistory365education.com*.

Grade 3
Works Cited

The 1619 Landing - Virginia's First Africans Report & FAQs. The 1619 Landing - Virginia's First Africans Report & FAQs | Hampton, VA - Official Website. (n.d.). https://www.hampton.gov/3580/The-1619-Landing-Report-FAQs.

A&E Networks Television. (2021, June 3). *Harriet Tubman*. Biography.com. https://www.biography.com/activist/harriet-tubman.

Adamo, D. T. (2015). Ancient Israelite and African proverbs as advice, reproach, warning, encouragement and explanation. *HTS Teologiese Studies / Theological Studies*, 71(3). https://doi.org/10.4102/hts.v71i3.2972

Adamo, D. T. (n.d.). *Ancient Israelite and African proverbs as advice, reproach, warning, encouragement and explanation*. HTS Theological Studies. http://www.scielo.org.za/scielo.php?script=sci_arttext&pid=S0259-94222015000100111.

All About Jazz. (n.d.). *All About Jazz Page Not Found*. All About Jazz. http://www.allaboutjazz.com/abriefhistoryoftheblues.

Ancient Africa. Ducksters. (n.d.). https://www.ducksters.com/history/africa/griots_storytellers.php.

Connelly, E. A. J. (2020, November 14). *60 years ago today, Ruby Bridges walked into history by integrating New Orleans schools*. New York Post. https://nypost.com/2020/11/14/ruby-bridges-made-history-by-integrating-new-orleans-schools/.

Documenting Slave Voyages. (n.d.). https://news.emory.edu/features/2019/06/slave-voyages/index.html.

DTugui, DTugui Delia is a writer who has a great passion for writing in-depth articles on various social issues. She has written both editorial and lengthy research pieces for numerous publications over the years. She lo, Delia is a writer who has a great passion for writing in-depth articles on various social issues. She has written both editorial and lengthy research pieces for numerous publications over the years. She loves her job and celebrates her accomplishments eve, & posts, V. all. (2018, October 8). *4 Famous African American Explorers You've Never Heard Of*. Black Excellence. https://blackexcellence.com/amous-african-american-explorers-youve-never-heard-of/.

Encyclopædia Britannica, inc. (n.d.). *African American folktale*. Encyclopædia Britannica. https://www.britannica.com/art/African-American-folktale.

Encyclopædia Britannica, inc. (n.d.). *Gullah*. Encyclopædia Britannica. http://www.britannica.com/topic/gullah-language.

Encyclopædia Britannica, inc. (n.d.). *Middle Passage*. Encyclopædia Britannica. https://www.britannica.com/topic/Middle-Passage-slave-trade.

Gates, H. L. (2021). *The Black Church: This Is Our Story, This Is Our Song*. Penguin Press.

Greenspan, J. (2019, October 30). *6 Strategies Harriet Tubman and Others Used to Escape Along the Underground Railroad*. History.com. https://www.history.com/news/underground-railroad-harriet-tubman-strategies.

Hayford, V. (2021, June 3). *The Humble History Of Soul Food • BLACK FOODIE. BLACK FOODIE*. https://www.blackfoodie.co/the-humble-history-of-soul-food.

Hill, R. (2019, October 23). *Marie Van Brittan Brown* (1922-1999) •. •. https://www.blackpast.org/african-american-history/brown-marie-van-brittan-1922-1999.

History.com Editors. (2009, October 14). *Black History Milestones: Timeline*. History.com. https://www.history.com/topics/black-history/black-history-milestones.

History.com Editors. (2009, October 29). *Underground Railroad*. History.com. https://www.history.com/topics/black-history/underground-railroad.

Ho, R. (2014, June 15). *How Slavery Affected African American Families*. Originalpeople.org. https://originalpeople.org/slavery-black-families.

How Slavery Affected African American Families, Freedom's Story, TeacherServe®, National Humanities Center. (n.d.). https://nationalhumanitiescenter.org/tserve/freedom/1609-1865/essays/aafamilies.htm.

How Slavery Affected African American Families, Freedom's Story, TeacherServe®, National Humanities Center. (n.d.). https://nationalhumanitiescenter.org/tserve/freedom/1609-1865/essays/aafamilies.htm.

Kendi, I. X., & Blain, K. N. (2021). *Four hundred souls: a community history of African America, 1619-2019*. The Bodley Head.

Lewis, P. (2016, March 7). *Who Invented Rock 'n' Roll? These Are the Black Pioneers Who Laid the Genre's Foundations*. Mic. https://www.mic.com/articles/136969/who-invented-rock-n-roll-these-are-the-black-pioneers-who-laid-the-genre-s-foundations.

Love, Z. (2021, February 1). *10 African and African American Folktales for Children*. The New York Public Library. https://www.nypl.org/blog/2017/02/01/10-african-and-african-american-folktales-celebrate-black-history-month.

Maranzani, B. (2013, May 31). *Harriet Tubman: 8 Facts About the Daring Abolitionist*. History.com. https://www.history.com/news/harriet-tubman-facts-daring-raid.

Miller, A. (2014, June 3). *African American cooks in the White House: Hiding in plain sight. The Washington Post*. https://www.washingtonpost.com/lifestyle/food/african-american-cooks-in-the-white-house-hiding-in-plain-sight/2014/06/02/c54cba10-e76a-11e3-afc6-a1dd9407abcf_story.html.

Milton, W., & Freeman, J. A. (2020). Black *history 365: an inclusive account of American history*. CGW365 Publishing.

Phillis Wheatley facts for kids. wiktionary:attestation. (n.d.). https://kids.kiddle.co/Phillis_Wheatley.

Pinchin, K. (2021, May 4). *How Slavery and African Food Traditions Shaped American Cooking. Culture*. https://www.nationalgeographic.com/culture/article/140301-african-american-food-history-slavery-south-cuisine-chefs.

Public Broadcasting Service. (n.d.). *10 Little Known Black History Facts*. PBS. https://www.pbs.org/black-culture/explore/10-black-history-little-known-facts/.

Regelski, C. (2021, January 17). *The Soul of Food*. US History Scene. https://ushistoryscene.com/article/slavery-southern-cuisine/.

Smithsonian Institution. (2013, February 13). *Poetry Matters: Phillis Wheatley, The Slave Girl Who Became a Literary Sensation*. Smithsonian.com. https://www.smithsonianmag.com/smithsonian-institution/poetry-matters-phillis-wheatley-the-slave-girl-who-became-a-literary-sensation-16722247/.

Soul Food: Origins of Soul Food. Research Guides. (n.d.). https://libguides.sunysccc.edu/c.php?g=67538&p=435812.

Stephen. (2019, April 10). Proverbicals! https://proverbicals.com/african-american.

Storyteller Jos Duncan re-tells African American Tale "The People Could Fly" at Jewish Seder. (2013). YouTube. https://youtu.be/n-RFj0hZU9E.

Thomas, R. (1970, January 1). AFRICAN EXPLORERS AND SETTLERS OF THE NEW WORLD. https://legacysunfoldingjourney.blogspot.com/2013/07/african-explorers-and-settlers-of-new.html.

Tidwell, C. (n.d.). Culture Definitions and Traits. https://www.andrews.edu/~tidwell/Culture.html.

U.S. Department of the Interior. (n.d.). *NPS Ethnography: African American Heritage & Ethnography*. National Parks Service. https://www.nps.gov/ethnography/aah/aaheritage/SpanishAmC.htm.

The Website Services & Coordination Staff, U. S. C. B. (1994, March 1). *The Great Migration, 1910 to 1970*. U.S. Census. https://www.census.gov/dataviz/visualizations/020/.

The Yale-New Haven Teachers Institute. Yale New Haven Teacher Institute. (1993, September 1). https://teachersinstitute.yale.edu/curriculum/units/1993/2/93.02.08.x.html.

Write...

Write...

Write...